Cultivating
Fruitfulness

Five Weeks of Prayer and Practice
for Congregations

Robert Schnase

Abii

Nashville

CULTIVATING FRUITFULNESS:
FIVE WEEKS OF PRAYER AND PRACTICE
FOR CONGREGATIONS

Copyright 2008 by Robert Schnase

This book is printed on acid-free paper.

Library of Congress Cataloging-in-Publication Data

Schnase, Robert C., 1957-
    Cultivating fruitfulness : five weeks of prayer and practice for congregations / by Robert C. Schnase.
        p. cm.
    ISBN 978-0-687-65433-8 (pbk. : alk. paper)
    1. Church group work. 2. Christian life. I. Title.

BV652.2.S36 2008
268'.434—dc22

                                    2008017081

All Scripture quotations unless noted otherwise are taken from the New Revised Standard Version of the Bible, copyright 1989, Division of Christian Education of the National Council of the Churches of Christ in the United States of America. Used by permission. All rights reserved.

Front Cover Art: Redouté, Pierre Joseph (1759-1840). Consignment : COA0065367 (Position : 1) Grenade, Grenadier punica - Pomegranate (Punica grantum). From "Choix des plus belles fleurs," by Redouté. Paris: 1827, pl. 67. Engraved by Victor. The LuEsther T. Mertz Library, The New York Botanical Garden, New York, NY, U.S.A.

08 09 10 11 12 13 14 15 16 17—10 9 8 7 6 5 4 3 2
MANUFACTURED IN THE UNITED STATES OF AMERICA

CONTENTS

WELCOME

Dear friends,

Welcome to *Cultivating Fruitfulness: Five Weeks of Prayer and Practice for Congregations*. For the next five weeks, you're invited to join in brief daily readings with everyone else in your congregation. You will be learning about the Five Practices of Fruitful Congregations—*Radical Hospitality, Passionate Worship, Intentional Faith Development, Risk-Taking Mission and Service,* and *Extravagant Generosity*. Through your daily meditations and prayers, you will be preparing yourself and your church for a deeper relationship with Christ.

Begin each of the five weeks by reading the definition of the practice. Each day is numbered; and other church members, friends, and pastors will read and pray over the same Scriptures and devotions as you.

Each day's reading begins with a Scripture verse and a brief devotion. Read thoughtfully, thinking about your own faith journey and your congregation's ministry. Each day also includes questions for reflection. Some people find it helpful to write their responses in a personal journal or to talk about these with a family member or friend. Each day includes a prayer that the entire congregation will be praying with you on the same day as you. And each day includes a "Challenge." Open your heart to the prompting of the Holy Spirit as you respond to the Challenges.

The Five Practices have transformed the lives of hundreds of congregations and thousands of Christian disciples. I pray that this book, supplemented by further conversation, teaching, and planning, can help your church become fruitful beyond measure for the purposes of Christ. And I pray that these five weeks may be a time of spiritual growth for you as we deepen the practices that help us follow Christ.

Yours in Christ,

Robert Schnase

The Practice of
RADICAL HOSPITALITY

Christian hospitality is the active desire to invite, welcome, receive, and care for those who are strangers so that they find a spiritual home and discover for themselves the unending richness of life in Christ.

Radical describes that which is drastically different from ordinary practices, outside the normal, that which exceeds expectations and goes the second mile.

Practicing *Radical Hospitality* means we offer the absolute utmost of ourselves, our creativity, and our abilities to offer the gracious invitation and welcome of Christ to others. We pray, plan, and work to invite others and help them feel welcome and to support them in their spiritual journeys.

Radical Hospitality
Day 1

Jesus said, "I was a stranger and
you welcomed me.... Just as you did it to one of the
least of these who are members of my family,
you did it to me." (Matthew 25:35, 40)

A YOUNG single mom stands awkwardly in the entryway with her
toddler, looking around at all the people she does not know on her
first visit to a church. An acquaintance at work casually mentioned
how she loved the music at her church and invited her to visit, but
now she is not so sure this was a good idea. She is wondering
about child care, self-conscious about the fussiness of her little
one, unsure where the bathroom is, too timid to ask directions,
doubting whether this is the right worship service for her, or
whether this is even the right church. Where is she to sit, what is
it going to feel like to sit alone with her child, and what if her little one makes too much noise? She feels the need for prayer; for
some connection to others; and for something to lift her above the
daily grind of her job, the unending bills, the conflicts with her
ex-husband, and her worries for her child.

Now, imagine what would happen if people took Jesus' words
seriously. They would look at this woman and the whole bundle
of hopes and anxieties, desires, and discomforts that she carries

and think, "This is a member of Jesus' family, and Jesus wants us to treat her as we would treat Jesus himself if he were here." With this in mind, what would be the quality of the welcome, the efforts to ease the awkwardness? What would be the enthusiasm to help, to serve, to graciously receive and support and encourage? Taking Jesus seriously changes congregational behavior.

Do you remember walking into your congregation for the very first time? What was it like? Who reached out to you?

Gracious God, give me a heart that
remembers the strangers who may be in my
path today. Help me share your
all-encompassing love with them, just as
you have shown love to me.

Challenge: If there are particular persons who helped you feel welcomed into your congregation, express your thanks to them personally or with a note. If that is no longer possible, give thanks for them by name to God.

Radical Hospitality
Day 2

"You shall also love the stranger, for you
were strangers in the land of Egypt."
(Deuteronomy 10:19)

RECENTLY I heard about a woman who was going through a rough time in her personal and professional life; and in her search for connections, hope, and direction, she began to visit a few churches. After her first two worship experiences to which she came alone, sat alone, and left alone without anyone speaking to her or greeting her, her prayer for her next visit to another church service was simply, "I only pray that someone speaks to me today."

What an indictment! Could that really happen to visitors in our congregation? The truth is, I've had that experience, even as a bishop! When I arrive at a church and start looking for the office, sometimes I pass by forty or fifty people with no one offering to help me find my way, despite my obviously being lost and my active searching for signs. At a few churches, I've had greeters offer perfunctory handshakes without even looking me in the eye, handing me a bulletin and pushing me along without any personal engagement or warmth. As my friend, Bishop Sally Dyck, reminded me, for the visitor or the person who is searching for spiritual help, "This Sunday is the only Sunday that counts."

In the same way stores sometimes employ agencies to provide "secret shoppers" to test the responsiveness of their employees, perhaps churches should consider working with a few conscientious members of another congregation, asking them to show up for worship and provide a "secret visitor" analysis. How are we doing at genuinely and authentically welcoming people? At helping people find their way? At providing worship leadership, bulletins, or other cues to help people who are unfamiliar with us to feel at home?

If a "secret visitor" came to your church, what would be the analysis? If this is the "only Sunday that counts," how do you respond to newcomers each week?

> Dear God, open my heart so that I can see
> people as Jesus sees them, and see Jesus in
> the people you bring into our community.
> Make me attentive to others, especially help
> me support the newcomer taking tentative
> steps toward you.

Challenge: Commit yourself to offering a simple and gracious word of greeting in worship to one person whom you do not know each week.

Radical Hospitality
Day 3

"… so that they may take hold of the life
that really is life." (1 Timothy 6:19)

Sometimes members forget that churches offer something people need. What do people need that congregations offer? Theologically, the answer may be "a relationship to God through Jesus Christ." This is too abstract for most, and for many it feels heavy-laden with negative experiences of intrusive and aggressive evangelistic styles. But the question persists. How do we express with integrity and clarity what we hope others receive? What do people need from the church?

People need to know God loves them, that they are of supreme value, and that their life has significance. People need to know that they are not alone; that when they face life's difficulties, they are surrounded by a community of grace; and that they do not have to figure out entirely for themselves how to cope with family tensions, self-doubts, periods of despair, economic reversal, and the temptations that hurt themselves or others. People need to know the peace that runs deeper than an absence of conflict, the hope that sustains them even through the most painful periods of grief, the sense of belonging that blesses them and stretches them and lifts them out of their own preoccupations. People need to learn how to offer and accept forgiveness and how to serve and be served. As a school for love, the church becomes a congregation where people learn from one another how to love. People need to know that life is not having something to live on but something to live for, that life comes not from taking for oneself but by giving of oneself. People need a sustaining sense of purpose.

How is your life enriched by being a follower of Jesus Christ? What have you received by being part of a community of faith?

"Grant, O Lord,
　　that what has been said with our lips we may
　　believe in our hearts, and that what we believe
　　in our hearts we may practice in our lives;
　　　through Jesus Christ our Lord. Amen."
—*John Hunter,* The United Methodist Book of Worship
(The United Methodist Publishing House, 1992)

Challenge: With a family member or friend, share your thoughts about these questions: "Why do people need Christ? Why do people need the church? Why do people need your particular congregation?" (Adam Hamilton, *Leading Beyond the Walls* [Abingdon Press, 2002]; p. 21).

Radical Hospitality
Day 4

> "Then [the king] said to his slaves,
> '... Go therefore into the main streets, and
> invite everyone you find to the wedding banquet.'"
> (Matthew 22:8-9)

When I worked in a clergy-training program at a hospital, I was called to the emergency room to support an older man whose wife had been brought to the hospital by ambulance. Shortly after I arrived in the small consultation room with the husband, a doctor approached him to announce that his wife had died. The doctor handed me an envelope that contained her wedding ring and eyeglasses to give to him. Needless to say, the man was stunned with grief. After a few minutes together, I offered to call his pastor. He did not have a pastor because they attended no church. I asked about any family members, and he told me his family was scattered across the country. I helped him with the paperwork, offered a prayer, handed him the envelope that contained the ring and glasses, escorted him to the exit, and watched him walk away alone to cope with the shocking news of his wife's death all on his own.

Life is not meant to be that way. God intends for people to live their lives interlaced by the grace of God with others, to know the gift and task of community from birth to death, to have faith to sustain them through times of joy and periods of desperate agony. Yet in most communities, forty to sixty percent of people have no church relationship. Many of our neighbors do not know a pastor to call when they face an unexpected grief. Most of our co-workers do not know the sustaining grace that a church offers.

Practicing hospitality is not inviting people to join a club in order to enhance revenue through dues. We invite people into that mysteriously sustaining community that finds its purpose in the life, death, and resurrection of Jesus Christ.

Have you ever invited someone who is not a part of a congregation to a service, ministry, or activity of your church? If so, how did it feel? If not, what has restrained you?

> Give me the courage, Lord, to offer your
> invitation and welcome. Give me the spirit,
> the grace, the right timing, the right tone, the right words.
> Give me the voice to fulfill the task you give me
> among the people with whom I live and work.

Challenge: Write down the names of three persons—neighbors, acquaintances, co-workers—who do not have a church home. Pray for them daily. Pray also for a time ripe to invite them to a ministry of your church.

Radical Hospitality
Day 5

"Welcome one another, therefore, just as Christ has
welcomed you, for the glory of God." (Romans 15:7)

ONE fast-growing suburban congregation practiced a dozen little
extra-effort details that helped them attract high-paced suburban
families. There were parking places for visitors, amiable and helpful greeters, brochures about a variety of ministries, an information
station, special electronics for the hearing impaired, a well-
supplied "cry room" for babies, and pagers for parents with
children in the nursery. There were also fresh-cut flowers in the
bathrooms and several seats with arms in the worship center for
seniors who need the extra push when standing up.

An urban African-American congregation announces before
receiving the offering that visitors shouldn't feel like they have
to give anything. "You're our guests, and we want you simply to
receive the blessings of this worship."

An open country church in a sparse rural county decided to honor
and show appreciation for a different special group of people one
day each month. First, they made sack lunches, added a personal
note of thanks, and delivered them to all the farmers for several
miles around. Next, they served volunteer fire fighters, and then

teachers. Over the year, more than a hundred people received these unexpected reminders of the hospitality of the church.

In all three churches, the pastor and congregation are focused on welcoming those from outside and inviting them inside. Paul implores the followers of Christ to practice an active hospitality. "Welcome one another, therefore, just as Christ has welcomed you, for the glory of God" (Romans 15:7). The grace received in Christ places upon Christians the joyful gift and challenging task of offering others the same welcome they themselves have received.

What does your congregation do to engage, invite, and welcome the unchurched? How do you personally help?

Dear Lord, you have embraced me with your
unmerited, gracious, and everlasting love.
Help me help my congregation to offer that same
love to others. Widen our vision and deepen
our commitment to serving you by serving others.

Challenge: Think about three specific ways your congregation reaches out to invite people and welcome newcomers. Think of three ideas about how you could help your congregation do better.

RADICAL HOSPITALITY
Day 6

Jesus says, "Whoever welcomes one such child
in my name, welcomes me." (Matthew 18:5)

IT IS easier to create a culture of hospitality in a building that itself communicates welcome. When Ann Mowery began her pastorate in a small, rural congregation in Missouri, attendance ran about 100 with a mix of ages, most of them older adults. After seven years, the attendance now regularly reaches 150 or more, and the congregation has built a new dining area and has renovated the youth room. The secret has been an active hospitality that has become contagious throughout the congregation.

For instance, when a visiting mom felt self-conscious whenever her baby started to fuss during worship, Ann met with congregational leaders and they decided that they valued having young people so highly that they had to do something to ease the discomfort. To show support for the young mom, they bought a comfortable, well-padded rocking chair and placed it just behind the last pew of the small sanctuary. Word spread to other young families, and soon they had to have two more rocking chairs to accommodate the moms who found this congregation to be the friendliest around! Rocking chairs for moms, a cool-looking youth room for young people, a new extension that makes the building handicapped accessible—the pastor and the congregation use these to help communicate the priority they place on welcoming more and younger people.

To become a vibrant, fruitful, growing congregation requires a change of attitudes, practices, and values. Good intentions are not enough. Too many churches want more young people as long as they act like old people, more newcomers as long as they act like old-timers. It takes practicing Radical Hospitality, and all the redirecting of energy and resources that comes with this. Churches can't keep doing things the way they have always done them. Little changes have big effects.

How willing are you to change your own attitudes and expectations so that your worship services and ministries could attract younger people?

Strengthen me, Lord, for the hard work of
hospitality with excellence and passion.

Challenge: Think of one simple idea to help your congregation make young people feel more welcome.

Radical Hospitality
Day 7

"For the love of Christ urges us on....
so we are ambassadors for Christ, since
God is making his appeal through us."
(2 Corinthians 5:14, 20)

RECENTLY I listened to the tape of Andy Stanley teaching about systems, and how systems trump mission statements. Mission statements may adorn the wall, but it's the behavior down the hall that shapes the church's mission. Stanley suggested that pastors and lay leadership consider a few simple, but challenging questions: What are three behaviors that you would want everyone in your church to practice—pastors, staff, volunteers, musicians, worship leaders, teachers, class members, church members, even visitors and guests? What are you doing systematically to motivate, teach, model, recognize, and reward that behavior?

Imagine a church staff or a lay leadership team that identified a few simple behaviors that they wanted everyone to practice, and then worked to shape the attitudes, values, and behaviors in a systematic, long-term way. Imagine a church that decided to focus on the guest/visitor experience and to cultivate the behavior so that everyone greets someone in a friendly, up-building way on every occasion of worship. Imagine if every adult class, youth ministry, mission team, and discipleship training taught, exemplified, and practiced the basic principles of making a stranger feel at home in our church.

The practice of the Radical Hospitality of Christ must move beyond the pastor, the worship leaders, the ushers and greeters and into the awareness of all our members and guests. The power of Radical Hospitality must run deep and wide and shape all our behaviors and responses for the church to fulfill its mission.

What are two or three behaviors your congregation could practice that would shape the culture of your congregation toward a hospitality that exceeds expectations? Are you practicing and encouraging these behaviors?

Our heavenly Father, cause us to be
what you have called us to be:
ambassadors for Christ.

Challenge: Radical Hospitality begins with a single heart, a movement from "they ought" to "I will." Take responsibility for inviting one person per month to a ministry of your church and for welcoming people you do not know. Pray for God to help you with confidence and genuineness and voice.

Reflections on Radical Hospitality

The Practice of

PASSIONATE WORSHIP

Worship describes those times we gather deliberately seeking to encounter God in Christ. God uses worship to transform lives, heal wounded souls, renew hope, shape decisions, provoke change, inspire compassion, and bind people to one another.

The word *passionate* expresses an intense desire, an ardent spirit, strong feelings, and the sense of heightened importance. It describes an emotional connection that goes beyond intellectual consent bringing eagerness, anticipation, expectancy, deep commitment, and belief.

Passionate Worship, whether traditional or contemporary, means an extraordinary eagerness to offer the best in worship, honoring God with excellence and with an unusual clarity about the purpose of connecting people to God. It is worship that is not dry, routine, or boring, keeping the form while lacking the spirit. It is not performance; it is devotion and celebration expressing our love of God.

Passionate Worship
Day 8

"Let my people go, so that
they may worship me." (Exodus 8:1)

UNDERSTANDING the meaning of worship requires looking beyond *what people do* to see with the eyes of faith *what God does*. God uses worship to transform lives, heal wounded souls, renew hope, shape decisions, provoke change, inspire compassion, and bind people to one another. We don't attend worship to squeeze God into our lives; we seek to meld our lives into God's. It's a time to think less about ourselves and more about faith, less about our personal agendas and more about God's will. We encounter a fresh vision of God's reality in Christ so that God's Spirit can reshape our lives and form us into the body of Christ.

Worship breathes life into the community of Christ's followers, forms identity, and provides a place of common learning about faith and listening to God. People express love for God, serve God, and experience God's gracious love offered freely. Worship forms communities, shapes souls, corrects self-interest, and binds people to each other and to God. God reaches out to us through worship services conducted in traditional and ancient forms or services marked with extraordinary spontaneity. God speaks to us in beautiful sanctuaries and simple buildings, in storefront gathering places and hospital chapels, outdoors under the open sky, and in the homes of members. In every imaginable setting, through worship, people seek to connect with God, allow God's Word to shape them, and offer their response of faith. God's Spirit changes us through worship.

What is your earliest positive memory of worship? What made it memorable and positive? Who was with you, and where were you? What did you learn?

Holy Father, help me to look beyond
myself and see the world through your eyes.
May I continually be changed
through my worship of you.

Challenge: Think about all the places where you have worshiped — buildings, chapels, outdoors, weddings, funerals, retreats. What do you think is God's intention for calling us to worship?

PASSIONATE WORSHIP
Day 9

"How lovely is your dwelling place,
O LORD of hosts! / My souls longs, indeed it faints
for the courts of the LORD." (Psalm 84:1-2)

THROUGH worship, God pardons sins, restores relationships, and changes lives. Jesus tells the story of the tax collector genuinely and humbly crying to God in the Temple and says, "I tell you, this man went down to his home justified" (Luke 18:14). Worship is the most likely setting for people to experience the renewed relationship with God that Christians call "justification," in which a person realizes that she or he is pardoned, forgiven, loved, and accepted by God. Worship is the church's optimum environment for conversion (the return to relationship with God) whether quick, dramatic, and memorable, or marked by gradual shaping and nuanced change over time. God expects lives to change in worship: attendees become disciples of Jesus Christ, and a crowd becomes the body of Christ.

The Psalmist describes an eagerness for relationship with God in worship, "My soul longs, indeed it faints for the courts of the LORD; / my heart and my flesh sing for joy to the living God.... / For a day in your courts is better than a thousand elsewhere" (Psalm 84:2, 10).

Through the relationship to God, cultivated in worship, the psalmist goes "from strength to strength" (Psalm 84:7), receiving the encouragement and daily renewal that characterizes life in God. People practice and experience resurrection in worship; every Sunday is a little Easter.

If you could extract all the worship experiences out of your life— all the sermons, Scriptures, hymns, prayers, fellowship you ever experienced—how would you be different? How has God used worship to change you and shape you?

Lord, cause us to be what you called us to be:
shaped by your Holy Spirit and changed
by our love for Christ.

Challenge: Take a bulletin or order of worship from a recent service at your church. Think about each part of the service— greetings, songs, prayers, sermons—and meditate on its purpose for connecting people to God.

PASSIONATE WORSHIP
Day 10

"You shall love the Lord your God with all your
heart, and with all your soul, and with all your
strength, and with all your mind; and your
neighbor as yourself." (Luke 10:27)

THE pastor, volunteer organist, and a few members of a small congregation met to plan what to do to deepen the worship life of the church. They spent an evening discussing the purpose of worship. They studied Scripture, prayed, read a chapter in a book about worship, and came to the conclusion that Christian worship is "for the love of God." Then they conscientiously considered what each person might do "for the love of God" to make Sunday worship more special.

They humbly opened themselves to creative change. One member volunteered to place fresh-cut flowers in the chancel each Sunday, "for the love of God." Another member volunteered to arrive early each Sunday "for the love of God" and go through the small sanctuary, wiping dust from the furnishings, arranging the hymnals, and cleaning up so that the sanctuary looked inviting and smelled fresh. The pastor decided that "for the love of God" he would prepare less formal sermons that would be more practical and useful for people. He'd also work on preaching with more eye contact and a more relaxed posture.

They decided that "for the love of God" they would close each service with everyone holding hands for prayer. They decided "for the love of God" to take Communion to the homebound whenever they celebrated the sacrament and that "for the love of God" they would talk to the Trustees about making the entry handicapped accessible. "For the love of God," the organist even agreed to support the soloist in singing with recorded music from time to time!

These little changes, appropriate to a small family-sized congregation, reveal how much the people care about worship, that it really matters to them, and that they really believe something is at stake in this sacred time.

What do you do "for the love of God" as a leader or participant that contributes to worship that is alive, engaging, and vital?

Renew us in our love for you, O God, so that
our worship is neither dry nor empty, but
full of devotion, eagerness, and joy.

Challenge: Pray for those who prepare and lead worship in your congregation—the pastor, musicians, readers, ushers, and others. Lift them before God daily this week.

PASSIONATE WORSHIP
Day 11

"I will sing to the LORD as long as I live;
I will sing praise to my God while I have being."
(Psalm 104:33)

ONE congregation had been offering the same program of Christmas Eve services for decades: an early evening service with Communion and a late evening candlelight service with high church music (mostly in Latin and German) that ended at midnight. The Communion services were sparsely attended but highly valued by church members, and the late service was well attended but seldom included many children because of the lateness of the hour. The church staff, after years of offering the same services, suddenly realized how few young families were attending on Christmas Eve. The formality of the Communion service made parents hesitate to bring their children, and many members had family guests with them on Christmas Eve from other denominations who were reluctant to attend Communion for their own denominational reasons.

After considerable conversation and planning, the staff decided to offer an early evening candlelight service designed for families, fifty minutes in length with blended styles of music. Immediately following this service, they offered a half-hour quiet, formal service of Communion for anyone desiring to remain and for anyone showing up especially for the sacrament. They continued to offer the late night service unchanged. In the first year, total attendance for Christmas Eve more than doubled; and the attendance in years since has doubled again.

Thankfully, the staff and congregation cared enough about worship to rethink, risk change, and develop new traditions that better serve the changing context and styles of younger worshipers.

Are there traditions in your worship services that leave people out or that make it difficult for some people to attend? What are some changes your congregation could make to welcome and include new worshipers?

Help me, Lord, with the hard task of thinking
not only about my own needs and tastes
so that we can consider how our worship
serves the needs of others.

Challenge: Ask yourself these questions: Have I attended worship weekly in the last month? Have I received Holy Communion? Have I practiced daily prayer? What is the most common excuse I use for neglecting the worship of God?

Passionate Worship
Day 12

"O sing to the LORD a new song,
for he has done marvelous things."
(Psalm 98:1)

A CONGREGATION that offered a single traditional Sunday morning service with about 300 in attendance decided to launch a contemporary service aimed at attracting and involving younger people. They consulted with other churches that had successfully launched similar services; sent visitors to other contemporary services; recruited a music team mostly from among their own congregation; and began planning with musicians, worship leaders, and volunteers to operate sound and video. The pastor decided to preach the same content as she preached for the traditional service but in a less formal teaching mode, using screens to highlight Scripture and key points. A core group of members committed to attend for a season, and the church publicized the new service and launched it in January. Three years later, attendance at the traditional service averages 275; and attendance at the contemporary service has grown to a consistent 135.

An older gentleman, his eyes watery with emotion, said, "I'd do anything to have my children and grandchildren in church again.

The church means everything to me, and it breaks my heart that my own family members don't attend anywhere." A friend responded, "You'd do anything? Would you listen to music that is not your style?" He answered, "I can't do that!"

Maybe people can't change their taste in music. But to reach younger generations, churches may need to offer worship in a variety of forms with a diversity of music. Supporting innovative styles of worship requires a spiritual maturity, a willingness to set aside long-standing tastes and preferences to encourage other people's quest for God.

Would you be willing to support, even briefly attend, a worship service that featured a style that wasn't your taste if it meant drawing others into God's presence? What is the value of this kind of support?

Help us in our congregation "to sing a new song
to the Lord," to be created and re-created
again and again by your Holy Spirit.

Challenge: Pray for the young people of your congregation and for the old, for the first-time visitors and long-term members, for learning from and teaching each other, and for the grace of shared worship.

PASSIONATE WORSHIP
Day 13

"Make a joyful noise to the LORD, all the
earth. Worship the LORD with gladness;
come into his presence with singing."
(Psalm 100:1-2)

IN SPIRITUALLY passionate communities, there's a palpable air of
expectancy as people gather for worship. Musicians, ushers,
greeters, and other hosts arrive early; and with care and eagerness
they prepare together, encouraging one another. They genuinely
delight in one another's presence, and they give attention to the
smallest of details to make the service go well for worshipers.

The gathering congregation, even when it includes many first-time
visitors, never feels like a crowd of strangers. There's a unifying anticipation, a gracious and welcoming texture to the way people
speak, act, and prepare. The pastor, music leaders, and worshipers
expect something important to take place, and they're eager to be
part of it. They expect God to speak to them while they experience
God's presence, forgiveness, hope, or direction. Singing together,
joining voices in prayer, listening to the Word, confessing sins, cel-
ebrating the sacraments, they intermingle their lives with each other,
and they connect to God. Expectancy pervades the congregation, the

active passion to serve God and to love one another. You can feel it. Authentic, engaging, life-changing worship derives from the experience of God's presence, the desire of worshipers for God's Word, and the changed heart people deliberately seek when they encounter Christ in the presence of other Christians. An hour of Passionate Worship changes all the other hours of the week.

In what ways does your congregation offer authentic and passionate worship experiences? How do you help? Do you feel a genuine eagerness to spend time in God's presence?

God who is near, may I always be eager to
offer you my very best. Let my worship be
authentic, alive, and marked with a
passionate longing for you.

Challenge: Learn to prepare your own heart before attending worship. Rather than looking for performance, search actively for what God desires to say to you through the music, prayers, Scripture, sermon, sacrament, and fellowship.

PASSIONATE WORSHIP
Day 14

"This is the day that the LORD has made;
let us rejoice and be glad in it."
(Psalm 118:24)

WHEN Meri Whitaker was assigned to Canterbury Chapel in the Oklahoma Indian Missionary Conference, the congregation had dwindled to a small group of older, highly committed women. They worked and prayed for some way to bring others into the life of the church. Immersing herself in the community, the pastor came to realize the dramatic need for Twelve-Step support groups based on the Alcoholics Anonymous recovery model. The congregation decided to take a risk and adapted their worship to complement and support the twelve steps. The worship service became a powerful center for testimony, decision, support, and transformation. The congregation now averages over a hundred people each week. Few United Methodist congregations are as acutely aware of the life-transforming power of worship as Canterbury Chapel.

Even with a thousand distinctive ways to worship, congregations marked by the quality of Passionate Worship stand apart. Worship is alive, engaging, appealing, and life changing; and leaders take seriously the importance of spiritual and practical preparation. People recognize that pastors and musicians love God and love worship. Leaders are clear about the purpose of connecting people to God and of God's desire to form people into the body of Christ. In whatever culture or context, Passionate Worship includes the "aha" moments that change people and mold them, the touch of transcendence that pulls them out of themselves, deepens their understanding of life and their relationship to God, and makes them feel richer, stronger, and truer to what God has created them to be.

Have you ever experienced an "aha" moment in worship? How did it change your worship life?

Open the eyes of my heart, Lord, so that I may see
your extraordinary presence among us in our
ordinary worship each week.

Challenge: Invite someone to worship. Do all that you can to make your congregation's worship a positive and life-changing experience for guests and other members.

Reflections on Passionate Worship

The Practice of

Intentional Faith Development

Intentional Faith Development refers to all the ministries that help us grow in faith outside of weekly worship: Bible studies, Sunday school, small groups, and retreats where we learn in the community of other Christians. By these practices we mature in faith; we grow in grace and in the knowledge and love of God. We pray that we are closer to Christ today than we were five years ago, and that by the grace of God, we may be closer to Christ five years from now than we are today.

Intentional refers to deliberate effort, purposeful action, and high priority. Growing in grace does not come without purposeful commitment to learning the faith and cultivating our love for God.

INTENTIONAL FAITH
DEVELOPMENT
Day 15

"They devoted themselves to the apostles'
teaching and fellowship, to the breaking of
bread and the prayers." (Acts 2:42)

LEARNING in community replicates the way Jesus deliberately taught his disciples. His followers grew in their understanding of God and matured in their awareness of God's will for their lives as they listened to Jesus' stories, instructions, and lessons while gathering around dinner tables, on hillsides, and at the Temple. Notice the dual reference to learning and community in the Scripture above. Jesus taught us to learn our faith this way.

In community there is a natural accountability. Covenanting together keeps us strong in our convictions and habits. That's why Jesus sent the disciples out two by two to go "to every town and place where he himself intended to go" (Luke 10:1). In pairs, the disciples could build each other up for the task; pray for one another; and support one another through the inevitable resistances, difficulties, misjudgments, and false starts. We learn in community because others keep us faithful to the task of growth in Christ. And we cannot learn spiritual qualities such as forgiveness, grace, love, justice, and humility by ourselves, but only by practicing our faith with others.

Churches that practice Intentional Faith Development offer high quality learning experiences that help people understand Scripture, faith, and life in the supportive nurture of caring relationships. Sunday school classes, Bible studies, short-term topical studies, support groups that apply faith to particular life challenges, children's church, vacation Bible school, camps, retreats, and youth fellowship groups are only a few of the countless ways by which churches help people probe God's will for their lives and for the world and bring people together to strengthen the body of Christ by building friendships and relationships. Christian disciples strive to develop faith and grow in Christ-likeness through study and learning, and God is best able to form disciples when people do this together and not by themselves.

Outside of worship, how do you deepen your understanding of the Christian faith? How do you cultivate your relationship with Christ?

Help me, Lord, to delight in learning your Word
so that like a tree planted by a stream of water,
my life may bear your fruit.

Challenge: Look at your church's newsletter, bulletin, or website; and count the ministries that help cultivate faith in children, youth, and adults. Pray for these ministries.

Intentional Faith
Development
Day 16

Jesus says, "Where two or three are gathered
in my name, I am there among them."
(Matthew 18:20)

A young woman pulls into the church parking lot just before the
session begins. She's running a little late. Her son carries his
schoolbooks into the church building. He'll work on homework
while Mom does her "Bible thing." She slips into the room as the
video begins. She and a friend had signed up for this, deciding to
"just do it" after years of wanting to study the Bible. The class also
includes two couples; two older women; a graduate student from
the university; and the leader, recently retired from the bank. She
didn't know most of these people before they signed up for
Disciple Bible Study, but she has been amazed at how much she
has learned from them as they've shared their thoughts about faith
and God and Scripture and at how much she's come to care for
them.

Every day for the past week, she has spent time reading Scripture,
sometimes lost in the archaic practices and customs and confused
by the stories and characters. She wasn't sure she had time for this

kind of study, and sometimes even now she thinks she's wasting her time. Then the leader talks about Moses' call—the bush, the fear and humility, and the excuses given to avoid doing what God asks. Her stomach tightens as she hears people tell about times they've felt called by God. She looks at her own notes from her reading through the week and sees the questions she wrote: "How does God call people? Sometimes I feel called, but I've never heard voices or seen burning bushes. Am I being called?" She shares her questions with others and discovers that they wrestle with the same thoughts. That evening, after she drives home with her son, she finds herself praying and asking, "What would you have me do, Lord?"

What is one learning experience in your faith life that has changed how you live in a significant way? How did you learn it? How have you shared it with others?

As I read and study your Word, Lord,
may I hear you speak to me.
Make me eager to learn your wisdom and
your will for my life.

Challenge: Somebody once said, "Everyone wants to want to read the Bible, but most do not." Think about the settings that have worked the best for you to learn from the Bible—personal, small group, class.

INTENTIONAL FAITH
DEVELOPMENT
Day 17

"So if anyone is in Christ, there is a new
creation: everything old has passed away;
see, everything has become new!"
(2 Corinthians 5:17)

THE song "Day by Day" from the musical *Godspell* expresses the
Christian disciple's desire to grow in the grace of Christ and to ad-
vance daily in the knowledge and love of God. In the musical, the
cast acts out the parable of the unforgiving servant (Matthew
18:23-35). After Jesus explains that his followers must forgive each
other from their hearts, the cast sings a beautiful prayer that asks
God for three things: "To see thee more clearly, love thee more
dearly, follow thee more nearly day by day" (*Godspell*, Stephen
Schwartz, 1973).

Growth in faith does not come easily or automatically but requires
placing ourselves in community to learn the faith with others. John
Wesley commended the practices of public and family prayers, the
searching of Scriptures, the receiving of Holy Communion, and
the practice of works of mercy—all in supportive community. We
learn the life of Christ and will of God by studying God's Word

and through experience with other people of faith. The early Methodist Class meetings, like modern-day Bible studies and effective Sunday school classes, provided the means to help people remain faithful in their journey toward Christ.

By joining a Bible study or class, we place ourselves in the circumstances that are most advantageous for growth in faith. Bible study is not just about self-improvement but about setting ourselves where God can shape us, intentionally opening ourselves to God's Word and call. God uses faith-to-faith relationships to change us.

Love, joy, peace, patience, kindness, generosity, faithfulness, gentleness, and self-control—these are the fruit of the Spirit. From whom are you learning these? To whom are you teaching them?

By your grace, O God, let every step I take
bring me one step closer to you.

Challenge: Thank a teacher of the faith in your congregation—a class or study leader, a pastor, a youth or children's volunteer.

INTENTIONAL FAITH
DEVELOPMENT
Day 18

"Let the same mind be in you that was
in Christ Jesus." (Philippians 2:5)

THE pastor of a small, open country congregation wrestled with
how best to provide opportunities for Bible study and fellowship
for members who have busy family schedules and live miles from
the church and from one another. Attempts to host weekday
evening studies at the church brought together the same few long-
time members who always attended faithfully. The pastor supported these efforts but particularly wanted to reach some of the
younger families who didn't participate as fully in such ministries.
One day she shared her dilemma and desire with one of the
younger families and casually asked whether the family would
consider hosting an hour-and-a-half study every other week in their
home if she could get a few other families to attend. The family en-
thusiastically agreed, and a few weeks later they had their first
home Bible study on a Tuesday night in the host's living room with
three other families present.

The pastor led an easygoing discussion with the adults and teens
about a chapter of Scripture and then led them in prayer together.

This worked so well that the pastor felt emboldened to ask another family on the other side of the county for the same favor of hosting a few others for Bible study. They graciously agreed. The pastor now leads two groups on alternate Tuesday evenings that reach about seven couples and families.

The pastor learned several lessons from her experience. First, people desire fellowship and want to learn about the faith, but they have trouble squeezing it into their lives. The more the church can do to accommodate, the better. Second, if congregations keep the end in mind—offering quality learning in community—their leaders may have to break out of usual patterns and expectations of place, frequency, and curriculum to reach people.

What initiatives are underway in your congregation to start new studies, small groups, or classes? How can you help? How are newcomers and those outside the church invited to these?

Help us with ministries that make Scriptures
come alive, O God, and help me open my own
heart to the instruction of your Holy Spirit
in the voices and examples of others.

Challenge: Commit yourself to participating in at least one small group, Bible study, or class during the next six months.

INTENTIONAL FAITH
DEVELOPMENT
Day 19

"Let each of you look not to your own interests,
but to the interests of others." (Philippians 2:4)

THE pastor and staff of a mid-sized congregation noticed that while the church received many new visitors, and a high percentage of them were joining the church, attendance remained steady month after month. The church practiced hospitality with excellence, with visitors and new members feeling welcomed at worship and into membership. But then after a few months, visitors and new members would become less consistent in attendance and fall away altogether. To understand the situation better, the pastor visited with some members who had recently joined. He discovered that people felt welcomed and supported when they first visited the church, and continued to feel a sense of belonging in worship. But when they tried to become part of Sunday school classes, choirs, and Bible studies, the groups felt cliquish and uninterested in welcoming new people. Even after months of trying, they felt at the margins in these smaller groups and ministries.

The pastor and staff soon realized that "the front door" was working well as people felt invited and welcomed. But they were slipping out "the back door" because too many of "the middle doors" were closed tight. They began a series of teaching events and lessons in the adult classes, service organizations, choirs, and Bible studies to move the culture of hospitality deeper into the life of the church. After some months, they noticed that the small groups began to grow and the worship attendance began to trend up again.

Congregations that practice Intentional Faith Development seek to cultivate growth in faith in intentional ways that address unmet needs and invite more people into formative relationships, habits, and practices that help people grow in the knowledge and love of God.

How is your church doing at offering opportunities for new people to feel welcomed, engaged? Are the "middle doors" open?

Teach us, Lord, to rely not on the wisdom
of the world or on our own understanding,
but on the truth you have shown us in Christ.
Help us open the doors of our hearts to you
as we open the doors of our church to others.

Challenge: If you are part of a class, study, choir, volunteer team, or support group, talk with your group about inviting new people in. And then invite someone new yourself!

INTENTIONAL FAITH
DEVELOPMENT
Day 20

"When Jesus saw him lying there and knew
that he had been there a long time, he said to him,
'Do you want to be made well?' " (John 5:6)

FOCUSING on personal spiritual discipline, Craig R. Dykstra says, "Christian practices are not activities we do to make something spiritual happen in our lives. Nor are they duties we undertake to be obedient to God. Rather, they are patterns of communal action that create openings in our lives where the grace, mercy, and presence of God may be made known to us. They are places where the power of God is experienced. In the end, these are not ultimately our practices but forms of participation in the practice of God" (http://www.practicingourfaith.org).

What Dykstra suggests about personal practices rings true also for practices of congregations. Practices shape us. Practices help us participate in God's work. Practices are the "doings," not just the good intentions, the thinking and theory and hoping and planning that occupy our minds and hearts.

When we talk about marks, characteristics, or qualities of fruitful congregations, we too easily fall into a "we have it or we don't" mode of thinking. I find it more helpful to speak of practices that any congregation can adopt, change, develop, begin, or improve upon. If we're not the kind of church we think God intends for us to become, we simply begin to act like it by adopting the practices until they help us become a new church.

The Greek word for the Book of Acts is *praxeis apostolon*, or Acts of the Apostles. *Praxeis* is the Greek word from which we derive the English word *practice*. Thus, the Book of Acts is about the happenings and doings of the early church! The practice of Intentional Faith Development puts us in the most advantageous place to perceive and receive God's activity and will for our lives. We become something new in Christ.

How can your congregation change the "values" of hospitality and faith development into the "practices" of Radical Hospitality and Intentional Faith Development? How will you help?

When my life is crowded with daily cares
and fears, Lord, help me make time to focus
on your words so that by the power of your Spirit,
I may walk forth in your light with confidence.

Challenge: Adopt a personal practice of Christian discipleship that creates an opening for God's mercy, grace, and presence to enter in, such as a weekly study with others or a daily time of prayer or reading.

INTENTIONAL FAITH
DEVELOPMENT
Day 21

"My Father is glorified by this, that you
bear much fruit and become my disciples."
(John 15:8)

A LARGER church tried unsuccessfully several times to launch a
new young adult Sunday school class. Church leaders were
stumped on how to get good quality teaching and fellowship going
for young adults. As they prepared for their next attempt, a married
couple in their mid-fifties stepped forward to offer their help. These
"empty-nesters" seemed unlikely candidates for teaching the class,
but they felt God had nudged them toward this ministry, they genuinely loved young adults, and they promised to give the class their
best time and energy. The pastor and staff approved their leadership, and the couple set to work. They contacted young adults and
couples to talk about their hopes for the class. They checked web-
sites, called other churches, and visited with other leaders of suc-
cessful programs for young adults to get more ideas.

Fifty to sixty people showed up for the first gathering; and the leaders described the purpose of the class, the topics they would begin
with, and some of the other activities and ministries they might do
together. From the beginning, the class began to demonstrate

extraordinary care for one another. The young adults adopted an invitational stance, always searching to bring others in. Within a few months, they were looking for service projects that could use the talents and passions of the members.

The class launched successfully, maintained strong attendance that continued to grow, developed an outward focus, and continues to serve large numbers of young adults today. Meanwhile, the church staff assessed how they could better meet the needs of other groups in the congregation.

What is one thing the pastors and staff learned through these experiences? Keep trying. Don't give up. Try different times, places, leaders, and formats, but keep trying.

Have you ever helped form a new Bible study, class, or house group? Would you like to? With whom could you speak who might also be interested? What's stopping you?

Help me, O God, to offer my gifts and talents to
your service in such a way that our congregation
may be a place where people of all ages grow in grace
and in the knowledge and love of your Word.

Challenge: Help your church start a new small group or Bible study, even if you are not a participant. Offer your prayers, your resources, your talents, or ideas.

Reflections on Intentional Faith Development

_____

_____

_____

_____

_____

_____

_____

_____

_____

_____

_____

_____

_____

_____

_____

_____

_____

The Practice of
RISK-TAKING
MISSION AND SERVICE

Mission and Service refers to the projects, efforts, and work people do to make a positive difference in the lives of others for the purposes of Christ, whether or not they will ever become part of the community of faith. *Mission and Service* includes activities such as clean up and reconstruction after disasters, after-school programs for at-risk children, food banks, and soup kitchens.

Risk-taking pushes us out of our comfort zone, stretching us beyond service to people we already know, exposing us to people, situations, and needs that we would never ordinarily encounter apart from our deliberate intention to serve Christ.

Risk-Taking Mission and Service involves the efforts to alleviate suffering and injustice to improve the conditions of others in the name of Christ.

RISK-TAKING
MISSION AND SERVICE
Day 22

"Do to others as you would have
them do to you." (Luke 6:31)

LUCAS runs a small business, has a young family, and volunteers
frequently at church. After a spiritually powerful experience on a
Walk to Emmaus retreat, he prayerfully searched for ways to respond to God's call to make a difference. He did not feel called to
ordained ministry, but he did want his life marked by greater service to Christ. He joined a team of men who met weekly for months
to plan a prison ministry, Kairos, to offer spiritual sustenance to
those serving time (kairosprisonministry.org). He and his team
signed security waivers and were permitted to spend seventy-two
hours in a maximum-security facility for violent offenders.

He describes the experience as nothing short of life changing for
himself as well as for many of the incarcerated and the other volunteers. Their significant engagement, genuine conversation, gracious respect, and active concern broke down barriers and
established relationships that would extend for years. The renewed
hope and deepened mutual understanding were little short of
miraculous.

The stretch of Christian discipleship is to love those for whom it is not automatic, easy, common, or accepted. Jesus stepped across oppressive social boundaries, intermingled with those who suffered crippling infirmities and social stigma, and offered hope to those at their point of gravest despair. He loved the least lovable and the most vulnerable, and he offered the same unmerited grace to the greatest sinner as to the finest saint. And Christ invites his disciples to follow him into this kind of love.

What is the most unexpected place to which your faith in Christ has taken you in order to make a difference in someone's life?

Give me grace, Lord, to risk comfort and
convenience to help someone in need in your name.

Challenge: Pray today for those in prison and for those who offer their service to make a positive difference in the lives of those who are incarcerated.

Risk-Taking Mission and Service
Day 23

"The Spirit of the Lord is upon me, because he
has anointed me to bring good news to the poor.
He has sent me to proclaim release to the
captives and recovery of sight to the blind, to let
the oppressed go free, to proclaim the year of the
Lord's favor." (Luke 4:18-19)

THE stories, teachings, and parables of Jesus consistently point
toward God's love for the poor, the sick, the outcast, and those
most vulnerable to the oppressions of society. Against the resistance of the religious elite and contrary to the advice of his disciples, Jesus lifts up the bent-over woman on the sabbath, touches the
unclean with healing power, releases the paralyzed from his bed,
eats with tax collectors in their homes, and risks the violence of
the mob to intervene for the woman caught in adultery. In teaching
and action, he shows that God's way includes costly demonstra-
tions of unexpected love to the least likely. The stories of the good
Samaritan, the father risking humiliation to welcome back his
prodigal son, and the rich person neglecting Lazarus at his own
doorstep all consistently show who Jesus is; and through Jesus, we
see what God intends for us.

The life of service flows naturally and inescapably from the teachings of Jesus Christ, and no congregation or disciple can avoid the direct gift and demand of God's call to love and serve others. Risk-Taking Mission and Service is one of the fundamental activities of church life that is so critical that failure to practice it in some form results in a deterioration of the church's vitality and ability to make disciples of Jesus Christ. When churches turn inward, using all resources for their own survival and caring only for their own people, then spiritual vitality wanes. When churches turn outward, they come alive with a sense of purpose and transform the lives of their members and the communities they serve.

What church outreach programs make the greatest impact on the lives of people in your community who are not a part of your church? How do you suppose your congregation is perceived by those in the community who have little power—the poor, the unemployed, the immigrant?

Lead us, we pray, in the ways of justice,
mercy, and peace. Inspire us to live for all,
to assist in ways open to us to alleviate
the suffering of others.

Challenge: List two critical unmet needs in your community that reveal brokenness and suffering. Pray for your church, or another, to find ways to make a difference.

RISK-TAKING MISSION AND SERVICE
Day 24

"You shall love your neighbor as yourself."
(Leviticus 19:18)

A PREDOMINANTLY Anglo congregation held an annual three-day home repair and construction project in poorer, predominantly Hispanic neighborhoods. For three days the targeted homes turned into work sites with dozens of volunteers arriving in SUVs, holding their Starbuck's cups, unloading high-cost tools, and talking on cell phones. Team members noticed that the families they were serving retreated more from the site and the workers each day. The volunteers became concerned about how the people who lived in the homes felt about this experience, so they contracted with Hispanic sociology students from a nearby university to do a follow-up visit to each of the families. The families reported feeling a loss of control about their homes, self-consciousness before their neighbors about receiving help from so many people, rejection at their efforts to assist in the repairs, and limited by language. They appreciated the work done on their homes, but they often felt invisible.

Based on these responses, church leaders radically revamped the program with far greater sensitivity and respect for the families they served, more intentional engagement, and mutual conversation in the residents' native language. Even the best-intentioned projects can benefit from evaluation.

Churches that practice Risk-Taking Mission and Service value engagement and long-term relationships. They measure the impact of their work in lives changed rather than in money sent or buildings constructed. Such congregations make sure that the people they serve feel respected, confident, and blessed, not dependent or helpless or indebted. They do *mission with* people of other cultures, not *ministry to* them. People come first, and Christ's love for people binds them to one another and to their task.

Have you personally helped with a hands-on, face-to-face service project that brought you into contact with people you would otherwise never know? What did you learn? How did the experience affect you?

> Father, help me distinguish between what is
> merely convenient and easy for me and
> what is essential for serving others with
> real love and respect.

Challenge: If you are a part of a Bible study, class, team, or choir, discuss the possibility of doing something that serves people beyond the congregation. Be bold.

RISK-TAKING
MISSION AND SERVICE
Day 25

"Truly I tell you, just as you did it to one of the
least of these who are members of my family,
you did it to me." (Matthew 25:40)

ONE United Methodist congregation had worked on service projects in Mexico for years, cooperating with the autonomous Methodist Church in that country, building houses and renovating churches. After Hurricane Katrina devastated New Orleans, the U.S. congregation felt called to prepare a team to help clean and rebuild. A pastor and congregation from Mexico also wanted to help. Together the two congregations, one from Texas and the other from Mexico, planned a work project comprised of volunteers from both countries. The joint work team coordinated with a Louisiana church, sleeping on floors, working clean up and repair during the days, and offering prayers and worship for local church members. The intermingling of cultures bore witness to the Spirit's ability to weave and strengthen life even during the most difficult of challenges.

Even when a small percentage of the membership immerse themselves in significant mission and service, the texture of church life changes, and the language of service and outreach begins to form conversations and priorities. Ministries of mercy and justice begin to take root. And these ministries become focused on changing lives and making a difference for the purposes of Christ. The interweaving of lives across culture, class, color, and age boundaries genuinely enriches the congregation and makes Scripture stories come alive in real experience. God strengthens the body of Christ through mission and service, and God empowers the body of Christ through witness.

How has a mission initiative or outreach ministry changed your church? How did you help? How did helping change you?

Thank you, Lord, for the community of faith
that has not only surrounded me with
steadfast love, but also called me to serve
others throughout the world.

Challenge: Learn more about what your congregation does in your community, your country, and the world through service and financial support to change lives. For instance, how does your church help people and learn from people in Africa, Latin America, or Asia?

RISK-TAKING
MISSION AND SERVICE
Day 26

"I was in prison and you visited me."
(Matthew 25:36)

DAVID, a pastor serving congregations and extension ministries for years, after conscientious prayer and study, concluded that capital punishment runs contrary to the teachings of Christ. He also realized how controversial and unpopular this perspective was in his own community. Public protest and signing petitions did not fit his style. Instead of trying to win consensus in his church about capital punishment (although he unapologetically teaches what he believes) and feeling frustrated by the intransigence of the criminal justice system and legislature to change, he decided to make his own personal commitment.

By patiently working through the resistance of the bureaucracy of a prison near his home, he received permission to make bi-weekly pastoral visits to one of the prison's death row inmates. Every other week, he submits to the security searches and completes the forms so that he can spend an hour in conversation, reading, Bible study, and prayer with a man convicted of murder who has no appeals, no options, and no hope as the world understands it. He does this consistently and without publicity or need for recognition. He holds no naïve hope of conversions or reprieve. He simply and graciously steps into the world of another person radically different from his own to offer the ministry of Christ.

Risk-Taking Mission and Service involves work that stretches people, causing them to do something for the good of others, that they would never have considered doing if it were not for their relationship with Christ and their desire to serve him.

What have you done recently to make a positive difference in the lives of others that you would not have done if it were not for your relationship to Christ?

Help us never to grow weary or discouraged
in seeking to love others as you have loved us,
even when we cannot see the signs
of change we hope for.

Challenge: Whatever critical issue pulls at your heart that seems unsolvable (violence, poverty, abuse, drugs, disease . . .), lift it up in prayer daily until some small way becomes clear for you about how you can help.

Risk-Taking
Mission and Service
Day 27

"What does the LORD require of you but to do
justice, and to love kindness, and to walk
humbly with your God?" (Micah 6:8)

AFTER their children went off to college, four women from a suburban congregation decided to move beyond their comfort zone with their volunteer spirit. They took a one-day training for literacy tutors, contacted the pastor of a mission church in an area with low-income housing and high dropout rate, and were introduced to several children and their mothers seeking basic literacy and English language classes. Each Friday, the four spent two hours teaching, listening, laughing, crying, and interweaving their lives with people they would otherwise never have come to know. They supported each other, worked as a team, made contacts that drew their own congregation into greater engagement with the mission church, and felt God's Spirit reshaping their perceptions about poverty, race, and language. It was a world they would never have considered entering if it were not for their relationship with Christ.

Serving others in this way takes us to another level in our understanding of Christian discipleship, moves us beyond our comfort

73

zone, and presses us to follow Christ into more adventurous encounters with people. Nobody returns from such service and looks at his or her own life in the same way. Intercultural experiences and genuine engagement with the poor have the effect of shining a light back on one's own culture; and extravagance, consumerism, materialism, and waste of abundance are seen in new ways. As we practice Risk-Taking Mission and Service, God's Spirit changes us, changes others, and changes our churches.

Are there others in your church who share a common concern with you with whom you can work together? What keeps you from stepping out and offering to help?

Teacher, help me along the path of
practicing Christ-centered service.
Remind me that though it is risky,
it is ultimately rewarding.

Challenge: Just do it. For Christ's sake!

Risk-Taking
Mission and Service
Day 28

"For those who want to save their life
will lose it, and those who lose their life
for my sake will save it." (Luke 9:24)

WHAT'S the opposite of risk-taking? Safe. Predictable. Comfortable. Certain. Convenient. Fearful. These words do not describe the ministry of Jesus Christ. Risk-Taking Mission and Service reminds us that congregations are not ends in themselves; they are resources God uses to change lives and transform the world.

God places congregations in a world troubled by many challenges. Schools struggle to provide basic education, and many children fall through the cracks. Criminal justice systems are overcrowded and do little to restore people to functional, positive participation in society. Medical services are overburdened and unprepared to serve unmet needs, especially of the poor and underserved. Immigration issues and environmental threats intensify fears. Drugs, alcohol abuse, gambling addictions, family violence, and poverty rob people of hope. A majority of the people with whom we share the world live with incredible uncertainty because of poverty, hunger, illness, or war.

As followers of Christ, we cannot live as if these things have nothing to do with us. Christ moves us closer to suffering, not further away. We cannot walk around obvious suffering, ignoring it like those who preceded the Samaritan down the road to Jericho. We can't moan about how somebody ought to do something. We cannot merely lift those who suffer in prayer, asking God to do for us what God created us to do for God.

Churches that practice Risk-Taking Mission and Service hear in the human need of their neighbors the distinct call of God. Against all odds, they figure out a response and offer themselves faithfully, even at some cost to themselves. God uses them to transform the world.

What are we asking God to do for us and others that God has created us to do for God?

God, whether I lead or follow,
help me to invite others to serve you.

Challenge: Is God calling you to make a difference, to serve, to help? Just say, "Yes!"

Reflections on Risk-Taking Mission and Service

The Practice of
EXTRAVAGANT GENEROSITY

Generosity describes the Christian's unselfish willingness to give in order to make a positive difference for the purposes of Christ.

Extravagant Generosity describes practices of sharing and giving that exceed all expectations and extend to unexpected measures.

Fruitful congregations thrive because of extraordinary sharing, willing sacrifice, and joyous giving out of love for God and neighbor. Such churches focus on the abundance of God's grace and emphasize the Christian's need to give rather than the church's need for money. In the spirit and manner of Christ, congregations that practice *Extravagant Generosity* explicitly talk about money in the Christian's walk of faith. They are driven to be generous by a high sense of mission and a keen desire to please God by making a positive difference in the world.

EXTRAVAGANT GENEROSITY
Day 29

"You will be enriched in every way for your
great generosity." (2 Corinthians 9:11)

SCRIPTURE is replete with examples and teachings that focus on possessions, wealth, giving, gifts, generosity, offerings, charity, sacrifice, and sharing with those in need. Giving is central to Jewish and Christian practice because people perceive that God is extravagantly generous, the giver of every good gift, the source of life and love. People give because they serve a giving God.

In the Old Testament, numerous passages underscore the significance of tithing (giving a tenth) and of first fruits (offering the first and best of harvest, livestock, and income to the purposes of God). And Jesus' teachings abound with tales of rich and poor, generous and shrewd, givers and takers, charitable and selfish, faithful and fearful. He commends the poor widow putting two coins in the treasury, giving out of her poverty (Luke 21:1-4). The story upsets expectations by pointing to proportion rather than amount as the measure of extravagance.

In the story of the farmer who built bigger barns, placing his trust too much in earthly possessions, Jesus reminds us, "Be on your guard against all kinds of greed" (Luke 12:13-21). Acquisitiveness does not foster a life rich in God.

And Jesus recounts the parable of the three servants entrusted with varying talents to illustrate God's desire for us to use faithfully, productively, and responsibly what has been entrusted to us. (Matthew 25:14-30). How people use what they have matters to God. Paul describes generosity as one of the fruit of the Spirit (Galatians 5:22). He describes how some people have the special spiritual gift of giving and generosity (Romans 12:6-8). All Christians practice generosity while some are particularly gifted by the Spirit to give in extraordinary measure.

From whom have you learned your patterns of giving? How do you feel about talking about your money and giving as an aspect of your faith journey?

Father, may I be generous to all your children.
Help me to give from the heart.

Challenge: Read from your Bible the passages referenced in today's reading from 2 Corinthians, Luke, Matthew, Galatians, and Romans. Why do you think Scripture focuses so much on wealth, greed, and generosity?

EXTRAVAGANT GENEROSITY
Day 30

"Take from among you an offering to the LORD;
let whoever is of a generous heart bring the
LORD's offering." (Exodus 35:5)

SIX members of the Finance Committee of a small congregation faced the challenge of paying for an unexpected air conditioning repair bill of $465. The church had already exceeded its maintenance budget for the year. The lay members included a retired salesman, a banker, a teacher, a housewife, a small business owner, and an insurance agent. They discussed options. Should they make an additional appeal for money on Sunday? Should they reallocate budgeted resources from other ministries? They considered fundraisers, such as a bake sale or a dinner.

As the meeting went on, frustrations grew. Finally, the teacher suggested they simply stop thinking so much and pause for silent prayer to see if God would provide another way. The others went along. After a few moments of silence, she looked around the room at her friends and fellow church members and said, "We all realize that any one of us could write a check for the full $465 and it would not make any major difference in our lifestyle or financial security." With that she pulled out her checkbook and wrote a check for $465 to the church. Then she said, "Anyone who wants to join me can add their check, too." Three others followed her lead and a couple of others wrote smaller checks. As a result of her inspiring and generous leadership, the air conditioning repair bill was paid; and an unexpected surplus of $1,695 was collected to launch new ministry initiatives!

There's no end to what the church can accomplish for the purposes of Christ when the sharp awareness of the assets, resources, and talents that God entrusts to us supercedes the fear of scarcity and the obsessive focus on needs and problems. Extravagant Generosity means graciously and responsibly placing ourselves and our resources in service to God.

Think of a particular time you enjoyed giving money. What made the experience delightful, memorable, and meaningful?

Gracious God, teach me to be generous
and joyful in my giving always.

Challenge: Think of a difference, large or small, that an extra gift by you could make in your church's ministry. Surprise yourself by giving an unexpected gift!

Extravagant Generosity
Day 31

"They are to do good, to be rich in good works,
generous, and ready to share, thus storing up for
themselves the treasure of a good foundation for
the future, so that they may take hold of the life
that really is life." (1 Timothy 6:18-19)

A PHILOSOPHY based principally upon materialism, acquisition, and possessions is not sufficient to live by, or to die by. At some point, followers of Jesus must decide whether they will listen to the wisdom of the world or to the wisdom of God.

Proportional giving and tithing force people to look at their earning, saving, and spending through God's eyes. It reminds them that their ultimate worth is derived from the assurance that they are children of God, created by God, and infinitely loved by God. God's eternal love revealed in Christ is the source of self-worth; true happiness and meaning are found in growing in grace and in the knowledge and love of God. Giving generously reprioritizes lives and helps people distinguish what is lasting, eternal, and of infinite value from what is temporary, illusory, and untrustworthy. The discipline of generous giving places people on the balcony, helping them look out at the consumerist society with new perspective, better able to see its traps, deceptions, and myths. The practice of generosity is a means by which God builds people up, strengthens their spirits, and equips them to serve God's purposes.

Tithing helps the followers of Jesus understand that all things belong to God and that, during their days on earth, followers are entrusted as stewards to use all they have and all they are in ways that glorify God.

What Christians *earn* belongs to God, and they should earn it honestly and in ways that serve purposes consistent with being followers of Christ. What Christians *spend* belongs to God; and they should use it wisely, not foolishly, on things that enhance life and do not diminish it. What they *save* belongs to God, and they should invest in ways that strengthen society. What Christians *give* belongs to God; and they need to give generously, extravagantly, and conscientiously in ways that strengthen the body of Christ.

Have you ever seriously considered tithing (giving a tenth to God)? Do you know anyone who tithes? What scares you about the thought? How would it change your life? Your church?

Strengthen me, O God, for the hard work
of being honest with myself as I seek
to practice Christ-centered generosity.

Challenge: Just for yourself, actually calculate the proportion of your income you give for God's purposes. Take your monthly giving and divide by your monthly income. Does the percentage surprise you? How do you feel about it?

Extravagant Generosity
Day 32

"They voluntarily gave according to their means,
and even beyond their means, begging us earnestly
for the privilege of sharing in this ministry
to the saints." (2 Corinthians 8:3-4)

A LONG-TIME member and proud grandfather stood at the baptismal font with his family for the baptism of his baby granddaughter. Another infant from another family that was new to the congregation was baptized at the same service. Following the service, the two families intermingled at the front of the church as they took turns having their pictures taken. At one point, the mother from the new family needed to get some things out of her bag, and the grandfather from the other family offered to hold her baby. Other church members commented on the grandfather with the baby; and he found himself saying several times, "Oh, this one isn't mine; I'm just holding him for a minute."

Monday morning the grandfather called the pastor at the church office and said, "I want to change my will to include the church, and I want to talk to you about how to do that." The pastor was stunned and couldn't help asking about what brought the grandfather to this decision. The older man's eyes grew moist as he said, "Yesterday I realized something while I was holding that other baby. I kept telling people that he wasn't my child, but then it dawned on me that he was part of my family, part of my church family. I've been a member of this church for more than forty years, and in God's eyes I'm a grandfather to more than just my own. I've taken care of my own children with my will, but I realized I also need to provide for the children of the church. So I want to divide my estate to leave a part to the church as if the church were one of my children."

Those who practice Extravagant Generosity have a God-given vision and faith to plant seeds for trees whose shade they will never see.

How have those who have come before you in your family, community, and church paved an easier road for you? How have you paved the road for those who will follow?

Help us put aside defensiveness and
self-deception to honestly look at our giving
through your eyes, O Lord.

Challenge: Think about the greatest gift you have ever received from being a follower of Christ and from life in your congregation. And then think about the greatest contribution you have ever made to the purposes of Christ and to your congregation. What do you want your legacy to be?

Extravagant Generosity
Day 33

"I am the one who searches minds and hearts . . ."
(Revelation 2:23)

IT IS through giving of ourselves as God has given to us that we help the body of Christ thrive. Offering our material resources to God is a fundamental activity that is so critical to the church's mission that failure to perform it in an exemplary way leads to decline.

Every sanctuary and chapel in which we have worshiped, every church organ that has lifted our spirits, every pew where we have sat, every Communion rail where we have knelt, every hymnal from which we have sung, every praise band that has touched our hearts, every church classroom where we have gathered with our friends, every church kitchen where our meals were prepared, every church van that has taken us to camp, every church camp we have ever attended—all are the fruit of someone's Extravagant Generosity.

We have been the recipients of grace upon grace. We are the heirs, the beneficiaries of those who came before us who were touched by the generosity of Christ enough to give graciously so that we could experience the truth of Christ for ourselves. We owe the same to generations to come.

Without the generosity of others, we would not have the tools of faith that have shaped our lives. We need to give back fully and extravagantly if the church is to continue to fulfill its mission. Extravagant Generosity is not just about the church's need to receive, but about the Christian's need to give. Generosity is an essential quality of spiritual maturity and growth. Generosity is a fruit of the spirit, a worthy spiritual aspiration.

How have you been the recipient of another person's extravagant generosity? Have you been the recipient of a congregation's extravagant generosity? Of God's?

By the generosity of your heart, O God,
all that we have comes to us by grace freely
given. Help us to give abundant evidence of
your love as we give generously of ourselves.

Challenge: Grow one step in your own personal giving. Develop a personal plan to grow in giving to God's purposes, of increasing the proportion of your generosity by at least one percent as you move toward the tithe.

Extravagant Generosity
Day 34

"For God so loved the world that he gave his only Son,
so that everyone who believes in him may not perish
but may have eternal life." (John 3:16)

A DOWNTOWN congregation in a moderately sized community had occasional transients and homeless persons who would ask for handouts. Often street people would be found sleeping on the front steps. The staff developed rules, guidelines, and policies for how to help or how to refer those who asked for help. They had many discussions about the pros and cons of giving cash, vouchers, and addresses of other social agencies.

As the pastor was leaving the church one afternoon, he noticed the part-time custodian carrying out the garbage to the large trash bin in the alley. There was a homeless person sprawled out beside the bin, looking barely conscious. As the custodian approached the trash bin, he set down the garbage bag he was carrying, pulled out his wallet, and removed a few dollar bills. Without having been asked, he walked over to the homeless person and gave him the money, said something, then continued his work and returned to the church. The pastor was amazed and humbled by this extraordinary display of generosity. The part-time janitor who earned less than anyone else on staff gave generously without even being asked, while the staff had spent hours trying to figure out policies and procedures.

The pastor asked the custodian why he gave the money without even being asked and also pressed him about whether he thought the homeless person might misuse the money for alcohol or drugs. "I always do that when I can," the janitor answered. "I give them a little money and say, God bless you, because I figure that they are some mother's son, some father's child, and so I give them something. What they do with the money—well, they have to answer to God about that. I just have to answer to God about what I do with mine."

Have you ever witnessed an extraordinary and unexpected act of generosity? How has another person's generosity influenced your own practice of giving? Who is learning from your examples of generosity?

Lord, help me to so live my life that others
see Christ in me. Help me to give in a
manner that cultivates and inspires
generosity in others in your name.

Challenge: This week, surprise someone in need by offering unexpected generosity.

EXTRAVAGANT GENEROSITY
Day 35

"And the things you have prepared,
whose will they be?" (Luke 12:20)

VIBRANT, fruitful, growing congregations practice Extravagant
Generosity. These churches teach, preach, and practice proportional giving with a goal toward tithing. They encourage their
church members to grow in the grace of giving as an essential practice of Christian discipleship; and as a congregation they practice
generosity by their extraordinary support for missions, connec-
tional ministries, and organizations that change people's lives.
They thrive with the joy of abundance rather than starve with a
fear of scarcity. They give joyously, generously, and consistently in
ways that enrich the souls of members and strengthen the ministries
of the church.

Like the other practices, our giving plays an essential role in our
fulfilling the mission of the church: to make disciples of Jesus
Christ for the transformation of the world.

Churches embrace newcomers with a sustaining sense of belonging when they practice Christ's Radical Hospitality. Through
Passionate Worship, God shapes hearts and minds, creating the
desire to grow in Christ. Through the practice of Intentional Faith

Development, people make themselves available to listen for God's Word and for the Spirit to mature their understanding of God's will. Inner spiritual growth finds outward expression in Risk-Taking Mission and Service as people respond to God's call to make a positive difference in the lives of others. As people grow in relationship to Christ, they grow also in the practice of Extravagant Generosity, offering more of themselves for the purposes of Christ and providing the resources that strengthen ministry and that help the church touch the lives of more and more people in the same way their own lives have been transformed by God.

How does your giving cultivate your own relationship to Christ? How does your giving build up the congregation, the body of Christ, so that the ministry of Jesus Christ thrives? Is there more you can do?

Lord, strengthen and bless our congregation
so that we may discover your presence anew
and change the lives of people you call us to
serve. Use me, even me, to build up the
congregation through the giving of my time,
effort, and gifts. Use me, Lord, for you.

Challenge: Pray for your church's ministry and for the courage, vision, and generosity to offer your utmost and highest to serve the purposes of Christ. Give yourself anew to Christ.

Reflections on Extravagant Generosity

_____

_____

_____

_____

_____

_____

_____

_____

_____

_____

_____

_____

_____

_____

_____

_____

_____

_____